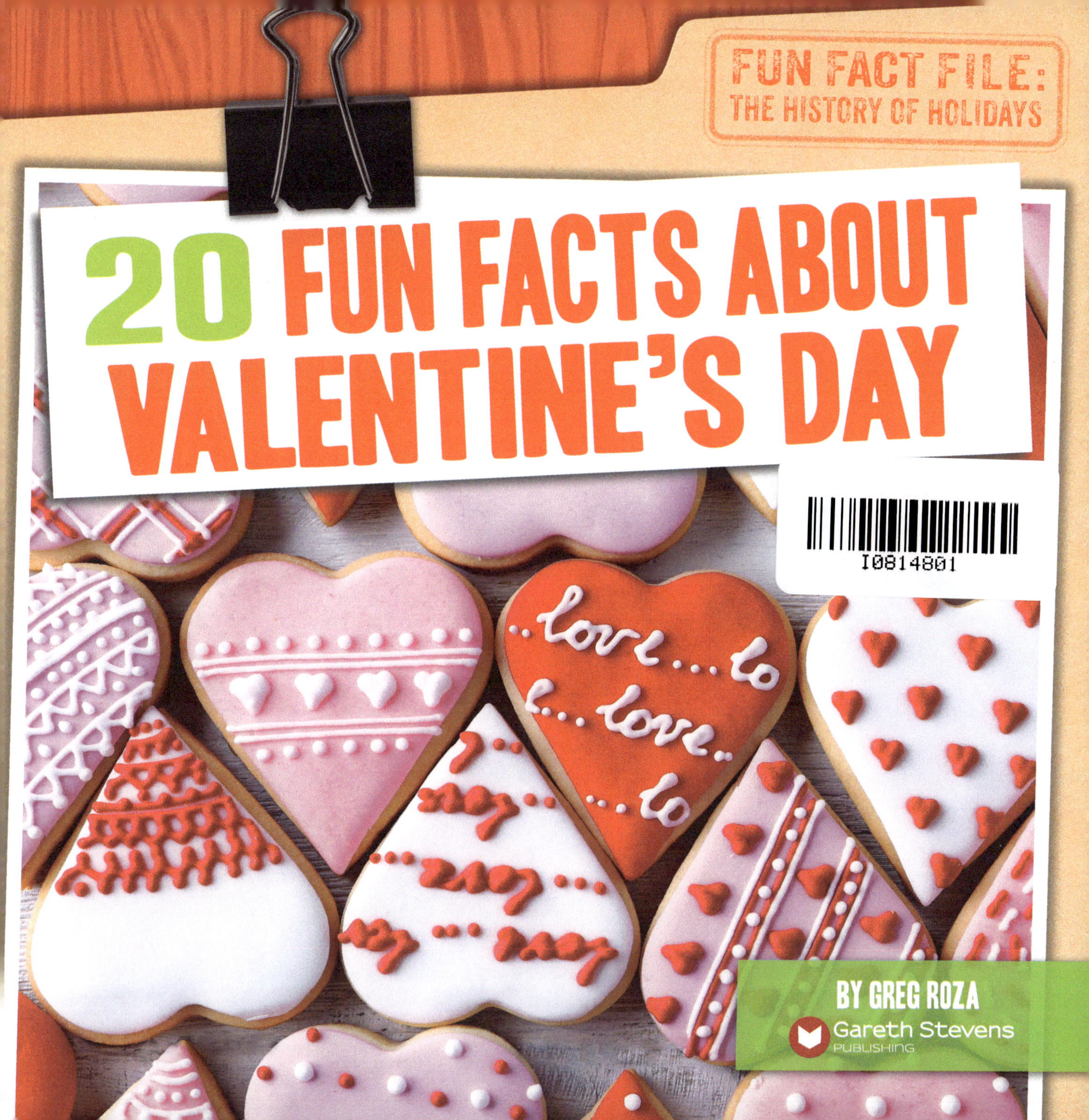
FUN FACT FILE:
THE HISTORY OF HOLIDAYS
20 FUN FACTS ABOUT VALENTINE'S DAY
I0814801
BY GREG ROZA
Gareth Stevens
PUBLISHING

Please visit our website, www.garethstevens.com. For a free color catalog of all our high-quality books, call toll free 1-800-542-2595 or fax 1-877-542-2596.

Library of Congress Cataloging-in-Publication Data
Names: Roza, Greg, author.
Title: 20 fun facts about Valentine's Day / Greg Roza.
Description: Buffalo, New York : Gareth Stevens Publishing, [2025] | Series: Fun fact file: the history of holidays | Includes index.
Identifiers: LCCN 2024003399 (print) | LCCN 2024003400 (ebook) | ISBN 9781482466287 (library binding) | ISBN 9781482466270 (paperback) | ISBN 9781482466294 (ebook)
Subjects: LCSH: Valentine's Day–History–Juvenile literature.
Classification: LCC GT4925 .R68 2025 (print) | LCC GT4925 (ebook) | DDC 394.2618–dc23/eng/20240208
LC record available at https://lccn.loc.gov/2024003399
LC ebook record available at https://lccn.loc.gov/2024003400

First Edition

Published in 2025 by
Gareth Stevens Publishing
2544 Clinton St
Buffalo, NY 14224

Editor: Therese Shea

Photo credits: Cover, p. 1 (main) Africa Studio/Shutterstock.com; file folder used throughout David Smart/Shutterstock.com; binder clip used throughout luckyraccoon/Shutterstock.com; wood grain background used throughout ARENA Creative/Shutterstock.com; p. 5 Irina Zharkova31/Shutterstock.com; p. 6 Camasei-lupercales-prado.jpg/Wikimedia Commons; p. 7 Sergey Goryachev/Shutterstock.com; p. 8 Pollaiolo, Piero del - Apollo and Daphne.jpg/WIkimedia Commons; p. 9 Pandora Pictures/Shutterstock.com; p. 10 Chissanuphong/Shutterstock.com; p. 11 courtesy of the Library of Congress; p. 12 Valentine-Epilepsy.jpg/Wikimedia Commons; p. 13 Stefania Valvola/Shutterstock.com; p. 14 Zvonimir Atletic/Shutterstock.com; p. 15 Adwo/Shutterstock.com; p. 16 Dave Z/Shutterstock.com; p. 17 Chaucer manuscrit portrait (détail).jpeg/Wikimedia Commons; p. 18 Oksana_Slepko/Shutterstock.com; p. 19 isfineday/Shutterstock.com; p. 20 (main) Ksenia Ragozina/Shutterstock.com; p. 20 (inset) Svetlana Siakki/Shutterstock.com; p. 21 1545GermanCardDeck.jpg/Wikimedia Commons; p. 22 Jmcanally/Shutterstock.com; p. 23 Brent Hofacker/Shutterstock.com; p. 24 StudioPortoSabbia/Shutterstock.com; p. 25 Esther Howland Valentine card, "Affection" ca. 1870s.jpg/Wikimedia Commons; p. 26 RYO Alexandre/Shutterstock.com; p. 27 (paper hearts) My Life Graphic/Shutterstock.com; p. 29 Evgeny Atamanenko/Shutterstock.com.

Printed in the United States of America

CPSIA compliance information: Batch #CS25GS: For further information contact Gareth Stevens, New York, New York at 1-800-542-2595.

CONTENTS

Words in the glossary appear in **bold** type the first time they are used in the text.

LOVE AND FUN IN FEBRUARY

Valentine's Day is **celebrated** on February 14 each year. It's a day for giving and receiving gifts from the people we love most! It also means fun activities in many schools.

What's your favorite part of this holiday? Some enjoy decorating with red hearts and cute cupids. Some enjoy giving their loved ones flowers. And of course, many enjoy the tradition of giving cards and candy to friends and family. Read on to learn how these and other **traditions** got their start.

A cupid is a figure that looks like a baby with wings. It's often holding a bow and arrow. It represents, or stands for, Cupid, the Roman god of love. That's why it's linked to Valentine's Day.

ROMAN ORIGINS

FUN FACT: 1

VALENTINE'S DAY HAD NOT-SO-FUN BEGINNINGS.

The **ancient** Romans held the Lupercalia feast around February 14. They believed certain actions chased away evil spirits and increased fertility, or the ability to have children. During Lupercalia, men killed goats and dogs to honor the god Lupercus.

This painting from around 1635 imagines Lupercalia. Men hit women with the hides of dead animals, believing it helped the women bear children.

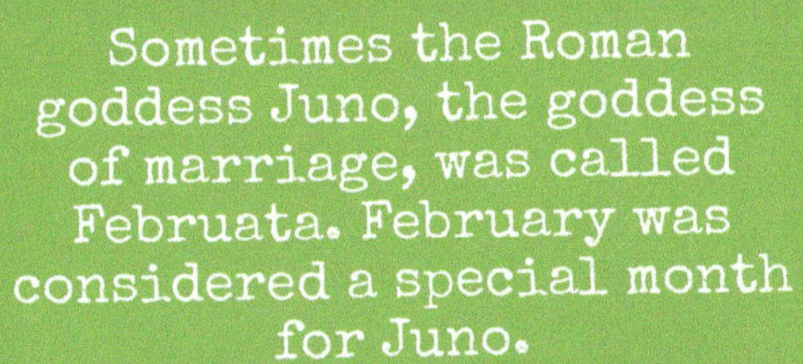

Sometimes the Roman goddess Juno, the goddess of marriage, was called Februata. February was considered a special month for Juno.

LUPERCALIA WAS SOMETIMES KNOWN AS *FEBRUATUS.*

The month "February" got its name from this Roman event. *Februa* is a Latin word meaning "purification," or the act of making something clean. Lupercalia, or Februatus, was a time in which Rome and Romans tried to purify themselves.

CAPTIVATED BY CUPID

FUN FACT: 3

In a Roman **myth**, Cupid shot a golden arrow at the god Apollo to make him fall in love with a female goddess named Daphne. Cupid hit Daphne with a lead arrow so she would hate Apollo.

Cupid was angry at Apollo because Apollo claimed he had a bigger bow. Daphne's father turned her into a tree to help her escape Apollo.

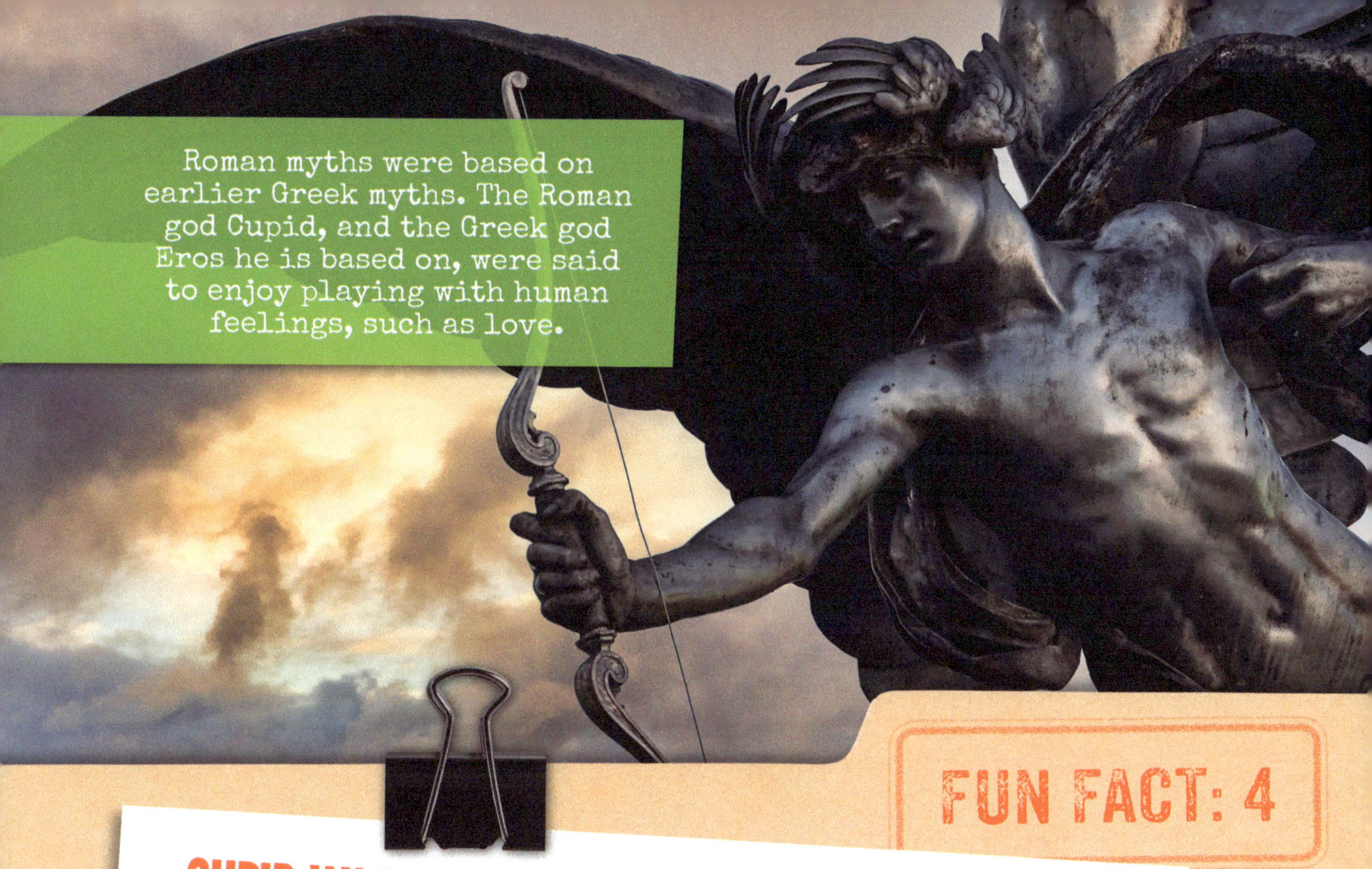

Roman myths were based on earlier Greek myths. The Roman god Cupid, and the Greek god Eros he is based on, were said to enjoy playing with human feelings, such as love.

FUN FACT: 4

CUPID WAS BASED ON THE GREEK GOD EROS, WHO WASN'T A CHILD.

Eros was a handsome and tricky young man. He had unlimited power and was unbeatable in battle. Eros used his powers to make people fall in love, and often to cause trouble.

FUN FACT: 5

CUPID WAS SOMETIMES CALLED AMOR, WHICH IS LATIN FOR "LOVE."

In fact, in Roman myths, Cupid was the son of the goddess of love, Venus. Venus, too, liked to make people fall in love. Sometimes Cupid helped her.

Paintings and statues of Cupid often show him with a playful look.

Tales of Eros, who became Cupid in Roman myths, go back to 700 BCE.

FUN FACT: 6

RENAISSANCE PAINTINGS OF CUPID INSPIRED EARLY VALENTINE'S DAY CARDS.

Many Renaissance painters showed Cupid as a young child. When companies started making Valentine's Day cards in the early 1800s, they used the **versions** of Cupid familiar to people.

WHO WAS SAINT VALENTINE?

FUN FACT: 7

VALENTINE'S DAY HONORED A CHRISTIAN SAINT—WHO WAS BEHEADED.

Christianity was new in the 200s CE. At this time, Roman leaders were trying to stop its spread. Valentine may have been a Christian who was beheaded, which means his head was cut off, on February 14, 270.

Christians are followers of Jesus Christ. Christianity was seen by some Roman leaders as a danger to their power and traditions.

One Saint Valentine was said to have helped Roman soldiers marry in secret—illegally.

FUN FACT: 8

THERE MAY HAVE BEEN MORE THAN ONE SAINT VALENTINE!

Beginning in the 1600s, Belgian **monks** kept records of the lives of Christian saints. More than one Saint Valentine died on February 14 in the 200s CE. Many believed it was the same person. But we can't be sure!

FUN FACT: 9

SAINT VALENTINE MAY HAVE SENT A LOVE NOTE FROM JAIL.

A tale about one Saint Valentine said he helped Christians escape Roman prisons, but was caught. He fell in love with his jailer's daughter. Before he was killed, he sent her a letter signed, "From your Valentine."

"From your Valentine" is sometimes printed on Valentine's Day cards today.

The Basilica di Santa Maria was built where a Roman temple once stood. It dates back to the 700s.

FUN FACT: 10

YOU CAN STILL SEE SAINT VALENTINE . . . KIND OF.

Many believe Saint Valentine's skull is in a glass case in a church in Rome, Italy, called the Basilica di Santa Maria. The skull is decorated with flowers. Other churches claim to have **relics** of Saint Valentine too.

A HOLIDAY OF LOVE

FUN FACT: 11

THE CHRISTIAN CHURCH CREATED SAINT VALENTINE'S DAY IN 496 CE.

Pope Gelasius I stopped Christians from celebrating Lupercalia. He named February 14 as Saint Valentine's Day, which we often shorten today to just Valentine's Day. In time, Lupercalia festivities faded. The holiday took on love-centered traditions.

The feast of Saint Valentine's Day, established by the pope, spread throughout the Christian world.

Valentine's Day didn't become a celebration of love until the 1300s. Writers such as Chaucer and William Shakespeare helped make this change happen.

FUN FACT: 12

ENGLISH POET GEOFFREY CHAUCER MAY HAVE BEEN THE FIRST TO LINK VALENTINE'S DAY WITH ROMANCE, OR BEING IN LOVE.

Chaucer wrote the poem "The Parelment of Foules" (or "The Parliament of Fowls") around 1380. It's about fowl, or birds, who had a meeting, or parliament, on Valentine's Day to choose mates.

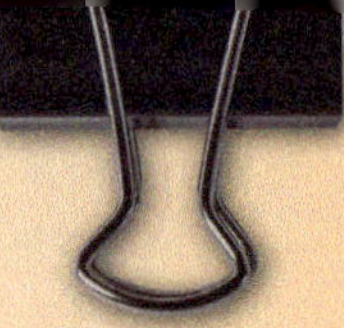

VALENTINE'S DAY ORIGINS

500S BCE The feast of Lupercalia begins to take place in ancient Rome.

200S CE The Roman Emperor Claudius II put Valentine (or more than one Valentine) to death on February 14.

496 Pope Gelasius I names February 14 as Saint Valentine's Day.

1380 English poet Geoffrey Chaucer writes "The Parlement of Foules," the first written work to link Valentine's Day and love.

1477 Margery Brewes of England writes the first known letter calling a loved one "Valentine."

LATE 1500S William Shakespeare includes Valentine's Day in his plays *A Midsummer Night's Dream* and *Hamlet*.

This timeline includes 2,000 years of Valentine's Day history, from Lupercalia to Shakespeare.

ROSES ARE RED . . .

FUN FACT: 13

YOU CAN SEND A MESSAGE WITH THE COLOR OF ROSES YOU GIVE ON VALENTINE'S DAY.

Mixing certain rose colors can have special meanings too. But some send roses just for their beauty!

Roses have been linked with love for a long time. A Greek myth told of the goddess of love, Aphrodite, creating the first roses. According to many people, red roses represent love, and yellow roses represent friendship.

Although red roses are the most popular flower to give as gifts on Valentine's Day, red carnations are the second most common flower. They're pretty and less costly.

FUN FACT: 14

RED ROSES ARE SO POPULAR IN THE UNITED STATES ON VALENTINE'S DAY THAT INTERNATIONAL FARMS PREPARE FOR IT.

Each year, nearly 250 million roses are grown in warm countries, such as Colombia, Ecuador, and Kenya. They're shipped to the United States for February 14.

HEARTS! CANDY! CANDY HEARTS!

FUN FACT: 15

THE HEART SHAPE—A CENTRAL PART OF VALENTINE'S DAY—IS ANCIENT.

Heart shapes showed up on playing cards in the 1400s.

It wasn't linked with the human heart and love until around the 1300s, though. The heart was once thought by some to be a place where memories of love were kept.

FUN FACT: 16

A PHARMACIST MADE THE FIRST VALENTINE'S DAY CANDY.

Oliver Chase, a Boston pharmacist, produced "lozenges"—thin, hard circles of mostly sugar and **medicine**. In 1847, he created a machine that made it easier to make lozenges. It became the first candy-making machine!

Chase named his company the New England Confectionary Company—or Necco. Necco Wafers are still sold today!

Oliver Chase's brother Daniel created a method of printing letters onto the candy hearts.

FUN FACT: 17

NECCO'S LOZENGES, NOW CALLED SWEETHEARTS, BECAME HEART SHAPED IN 1902. THEY'VE BEEN SOLD EVERY YEAR SINCE—EXCEPT FOR ONE!

There were no Sweethearts in 2019. The Necco company had failed, but the Spangler Candy Company then bought it. Sweethearts were on sale for Valentine's Day 2020.

Cadbury might have been the first to make heart-shaped boxes, but other companies quickly followed.

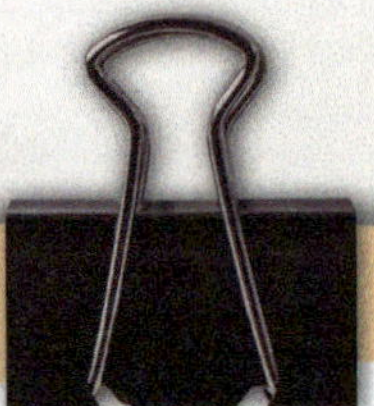

FUN FACT: 18

THE YEAR 1861 WAS AN IMPORTANT DATE IN THE HISTORY OF VALENTINE'S DAY CANDY.

That year, British chocolate maker Richard Cadbury came up with an idea. He created heart-shaped boxes for Cadbury chocolates. The boxes could store small things once the chocolates were eaten.

BE MY VALENTINE

FUN FACT: 19

IN 1849, ESTHER HOWLAND BEGAN MAKING AND SELLING THE FIRST **MASS-PRODUCED** VALENTINE CARDS IN THE UNITED STATES.

Howland became known as the "Mother of the Valentine."

In her home in Worcester, Massachusetts, Howland used lace, ribbons, and colorful drawings for her first cards. Her business grew. At its most successful, it made $100,000 a year!

FUN FACT: 20

AMERICANS BUY ABOUT 145 MILLION VALENTINE'S DAY CARDS EACH YEAR TO SEND TO LOVED ONES.

And that doesn't even include valentines that students give each other in school! Christmas is the only holiday when more greeting cards are purchased.

In 2022, Americans spent $23.9 billion on Valentine's Day.

MORE FUN VALENTINE'S DAY FACTS

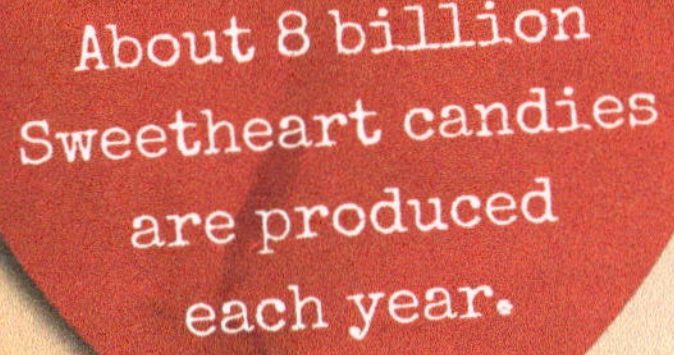

About 8 billion Sweetheart candies are produced each year.

Americans spent about $751.3 million on Valentine's Day gifts for their pets in 2020.

Europeans and Americans began giving cards on Valentine's Day in the 1700s.

More than 36 million heart-shaped boxes of chocolates are sold every year.

There are three U.S. cities with the name Valentine (in Arizona, Nebraska, and Texas) and a city named Valentines in Virginia.

In the Philippines, many people get married at the same time on Valentine's Day.

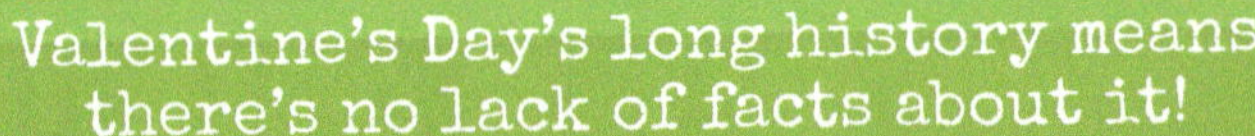

Valentine's Day's long history means there's no lack of facts about it!

A HOLIDAY WITH HEART

Valentine's Day has a surprisingly long and colorful history. We've come a long way from ancient traditions and Christian saints to heart-shaped sweets and Valentine's Day cards.

Today's Valentine's Day is just as much about celebrating friendship as it is about love. As the years go by, traditions will no doubt change, as they have in the past. Hopefully this holiday will continue to be about making a special person's day sweeter with thoughtful and kind actions.

If you don't have Valentine's Day traditions in your family, start some traditions next February 14!

GLOSSARY

ancient: Describing something from a very long time ago.

celebrate: To show happiness for an event through activities such as eating or playing music.

inspire: To cause someone to want to do something.

mass-produce: To make a number of the same thing, often using machines.

medicine: A drug taken to make a sick person well.

monk: A man in a religious community who makes vows, or promises, such as to remain poor, unmarried, and away from the outside world.

myth: A story that was told by a people to explain a practice, belief, or natural event.

pharmacist: Someone trained to identify, measure, and provide medicines.

relic: An object treated with great respect because of its connection to a saint.

Renaissance: The period of European history between the 14th and 17th centuries marked by an increase in art and literature, inspired by ancient times and by the beginnings of modern science.

tradition: A way of life or an action that a group of people has practiced for a long time.

version: A form of something that is different from others.

FOR MORE INFORMATION

BOOKS

Jelinek, KeriAnne N. *What Is Valentine's Day?* Du Bois, PA: Sloth Dreams Books & Publishing, 2023.

Rossow, Kayla. *Make Your Own Valentine's Day Crafts.* Mankato, MN: Black Rabbit Books, 2024.

Sabelko, Rebecca. *Valentine's Day.* Minneapolis, MN: Bellwether Media, Inc., 2024.

WEBSITES

43 Valentine's Day Recipes to Make with Kids
www.food.com/ideas/valentine-kids-recipes-7085#c-861448
Find a recipe you can make with an adult for Valentine's Day.

Holidays: Valentine's Day
www.ducksters.com/holidays/valentines_day.php
This site helps you review and learn more interesting facts about Valentine's Day.

7 Unique Valentine's Day Traditions
www.history.com/news/valentines-day-traditions
Read about Valentine's Day traditions in different countries.

Publisher's note to educators and parents: Our editors have carefully reviewed these websites to ensure that they are suitable for students. Many websites change frequently, however, and we cannot guarantee that a site's future contents will continue to meet our high standards of quality and educational value. Be advised that students should be closely supervised whenever they access the internet.

INDEX